To Keep Love Blurry

To Keep Love Blurry

Poems by

C̶r̶a̶i̶g̶ ̶M̶o̶r̶g̶a̶n̶ Teicher

American Poets Continuum Series, No. 135

BOA Editions, Ltd. ▫ Rochester, NY ▫ 2012

First Edition
12 13 14 15   7 6 5 4 3 2 1

For information about permission to reuse any material from this book, please contact
The Permissions Company at www.permissionscompany.com or e-mail permdude@
eclipse.net.

Publications by BOA Editions, Ltd.—a not-for-profit corporation
under section 501 (c) (3) of the United States Internal Revenue
Code—are made possible with funds from a variety of sources,
including public funds from the New York State Council on the
Arts, a state agency; the Literature Program of the National En-
dowment for the Arts; the County of Monroe, NY; the Lannan
Foundation for support of the Lannan Translations Selection Se-
ries; the Mary S. Mulligan Charitable Trust; the Rochester Area
Community Foundation; the Arts & Cultural Council for Greater
Rochester; the Steeple-JackFund; the Ames-Amzalak Memorial Trust in memory of Henry
Ames, Semon Amzalak and Dan Amzalak; and contributions from many individuals na-
tionwide. See Colophon on page 112 for special individual acknowledgments.

ART WORKS.
arts.gov

State of the Arts

NYSCA

Cover Design: Sandy Knight
Cover Art: Jorge Queiroz
Interior Design and Composition: Richard Foerster
Manufacturing: McNaughton & Gunn
BOA Logo: Mirko

Library of Congress Cataloging-in-Publication Data

Teicher, Craig Morgan, 1979–
To keep love blurry : poems / by Craig Morgan Teicher. — 1st ed.
    p. cm. — (American Poets Continuum Series ; 135)
Includes bibliographical references.
ISBN 978-1-934414-93-4 (pbk. : alk. paper)
I. Title.
PS3620.E4359T65 2012
811'.6—dc23
                        2012014339

BOA Editions, Ltd.
250 North Goodman Street, Suite 306
Rochester, NY 14607
www.boaeditions.org
A. Poulin, Jr., Founder (1938–1996)

For Cal and Simone—you should know that it's a lot more fun than these poems suggest—

and

for Brenda, who knows...

Contents

Part Four

I

II

BOOK TWO: A CELEBRATION

⊞

BOOK ONE: LIFE STUDIES

*"Those blessèd structures, plot and rhyme—
why are they no help to me now..."*
　　　　　　　　—Robert Lowell

*"so many things seem filled with the intent
to be lost..."*
　　　　　　　　—Elizabeth Bishop

"They are more fathers than sons themselves now."
　　　　　　　　—Donald Justice

PART ONE

The Prince of Rivers

In the land of rivers I was the prince of rivers.
In the land of houses I lived in a thousand houses.
In the land of scattered bones my bones were scattered

by worshipful princes who carried each one like a scepter.
I was there and a breeze eddied around me.
In the land of questions I was the subject of questions.

I'm sorry what was lost was found utterly changed.
I could see through the sky and bring down the lonely stars.
When I was happy, lambs were born. They stood up

enacting their first dance of balance. In the land of frost
I was never cold. A warm breeze eddied around me.
When I thundered the sky tore like paper. Beyond the sky

the sky tore and rain fell into the moon's dark holes.
In the land of eagles I received messages from eagles.
I'm sorry the moon is a fake gray plate. I'm sorry the day

is so dark. In the land of the future I saw men of stone.
When I was sad all the seas swelled. The islands
were swallowed and forgotten; books were drenched and forgotten.

When I was old my hair was as long as my story.
I'm sorry the branch bearing fruit is so high.
When I was young trees arched toward me like I was the sun.

I'm sorry the dead are quiet as ash. I'm sorry what's left is so cold.
I knew I could escape through a hole in the sky. Wherever
I wept thick stalks grew. I knew I could weep for a long time to come.

Father

"You think too much—it's what I've always said.
There's nothing new you'll find by looking in your head,
no encoded family secrets, no incestuous kiss
from a molested aunt. It's just exactly this,
just memories less in focus when remembered again,
modified, chipped into kindling for fear—
I've spent most of my life afraid, being unclear
about whether an honest mistake counts as a sin,
and what the consequences were of hurtful things I did.
There are no big answers, no revelations.
Isn't my life proof enough that anything I hid
I lost? I'll die, and so will you, without explanations.
I'm no model, but do go for things you can touch—
souvenir snow globes, girls. You think too much."

Mother

"'I'm dead, I'm dead, I'm dead, I'm dead'—you've said
so so many times. You wear my death like a birthmark.
It's not what I intended, but I do let it go to my head
occasionally. God knows I was modest in life.
But is my death enough to motor all your days, to spark
enough imagination and verve to sustain your son and wife?
Does it really excite you and keep you awake
to the world at hand? Maybe. You've managed to make
a little name for yourself, and you're funny,
which is a surprise. You were always a good writer,
so nothing's shocking there, and you even make some money!
But obsessing over me—I'm afraid it keeps you slighter…
But this is not the kind of stuff *I* would have said.
It's your call. This is you talking to you—I'm dead."

Confession

Lowell did it best because he understood
that even when his art was saying *I've been bad,*
he had to make himself look good.
No one loves a truly self-loathing lad,
though one and all are charmed
by a man's interest in his own evil,
which he puts on show for those he's harmed
or those who haven't been but hope they will
be. Daredevil, rock star, martyr-circus-freak,
he sets himself on fire every night,
doused later as the audience cries, *how unique.*
It's a trick they like; he's perfectly alright,
because he's in love with himself, playing hate.
True self-haters perform to empty houses, late.

It Came from the Primordial Ooze

The mind is so big it's easy to get lost in thought,
    big as a grapefruit, or like an astonishing
    house bigger on the inside than its frame
    could possibly contain. I remember something

I'd forgot and wonder what it got lost behind,
    beneath, around, about. Books are divided
    into pages, stacked and bound, because no one
    can read one all at once, hence chapters

and why a good song is just three minutes long,
    as if a kind of mind can only think
    so much, which explains why an octopus
    can learn to open a jar but not drive a car.

A voice answers most questions the self asks
    the self, but where does he go when
    the self says I know? If I write down everything
    I think and string the sentences end to end,

how many times around the world can I wrap my mind?
    The caption says a blue whale has a heart
    as big as a Volkswagen, and the photo below
    makes him look kind. A man has a heart

as small as a ball that pumps blood for miles
    and feels what the mind can't understand,
    while the mind mixes its metaphors to
    outdistance the reach of the hand.

Action Reaction

My actions define me—is that true?
Or am I saved by the helpful notion
that I'm good by nature, despite what I do?

What if I'm forced to do something I don't want to?
Or practically forced—coerced. The unceasing promotion
of the idea we have control—is that *ever* true?

Like what if it's not my act but evil that might ensue?
Am I accountable for some disaster I unwittingly set in motion?
Not if I'm good by nature, despite what I do...

Even if I knowingly did wrong and, without apology, flew,
shouldn't deeper love of me inspire devotion?
If my actions define me isn't it also true

that love should redeem? Otherwise, why favor virtue?
Why not shrug and say I'm susceptible to every emotion
by nature—often I can't control what I do

and had no say, of course, in the cards I drew.
Wrong and right choices are alike as drops in an ocean.
Contradiction defines me—that's obviously true,
even if nature made me good. *Does* it matter what I do?

*Variations on the Moment of Apprehending the Extent
of One's Responsibilities*

1

that minute subdivision of time
during which the full consequence

flickers, just before the door clicks
shut but just after you could have

stopped it from shutting, when
you realize, your hand already

seizing your empty pocket, that
you have left your keys inside

2

that useless subdivision of time
in which what really happens

could never have been
prevented—it yawns so wide

though you can barely fit
a blink into it, like the moment

just before the door clicks shut
but just after you realize

3

you have left your keys inside.
So many things are unsatisfactory,

like the moment, like the baby
monitor, like your hand already

seizing your empty pocket,
useless. Consequence

flickers, what really happens
could fit behind a blink

4

that useless subdivision of time
in which what happens could fit,

flickers, could never have been
prevented, is so unsatisfactory

like the moment just before
the door clicks shut but just after

you could have stopped it from
closing with the back of your foot

5

your hand already seizing
your empty pocket, as if you could

go back, your keys inside,
and begin again, take your clothes

off, crawl back, deep into bed.
So many things are unsatisfactory—

that you have left your keys inside,
that *this* is when you realize

6

this could never have been
prevented, that what you realize

is not only useless but infinitely
painful, because minute,

irrevocable, like the baby
who flickers in the video monitor,

a blink in which the door clicks shut.
You could never have stopped it

7

till now, just after you realize
so many things are unsatisfactory,

just before, your hand already
seizing your empty pocket,

the full consequence flickers
behind a blink that is now

your measure of time, useless
because it already happened.

Motherhood

Was my mother very beautiful? No, not especially.
So why did I always seek out very pretty girls
with pillowy breasts and curves to mother me?
My desire cross-wired with a son's need for care,
which might explain my mother-hunting in the curls
of redheads' and brunettes' hair.
I'm giddy to talk about my losses and pain
—plain and hurt is hotter than merely plain—
as if to say *take your time, listen, bandage me;*
I'm bleeding now, but don't rush, I will always be.
I never got laid with lines like these, which was the way
I think it was supposed to work, like it would betray
my mother to actually have a lover. But don't worry,
I'm married now, the conventional way to keep love blurry.

Anger

Before meeting you, I had never been as angry
as I get in our weekly fight. Was all that bile
always simmering in me, my pressurized vial
of hell awaiting an excuse to blow? You set free
something mean, something that likes to hurt.
Fighting is exciting; it makes fire from doubt.
Of course, I'm also copying you—your curt
reply to whatever I say, followed by a bout
of crazed yelling—barely hidden, our worst
selves leap giddily out, and if we're both ashamed,
we'd never say so, unless the other says so first.
But no harm done after a day or two. I've blamed
you, but I'm grateful, really. When we fight,
like a tantrum-fresh child, I'm powerful, alive, right.

PART TWO

On His Bed and No Longer Among the Living

1

Reading and writing are much the same activity: words employed to carry some part of the world or the mind across the divide that separates the two. When I want to write, I read, and when I want to read, I write, so I have been reading *The Rings of Saturn* by W. G. Sebald. Sebald's novel is a kind of travelogue that follows a journey through English towns, recounting the events and thoughts that preoccupy the traveler. The boundaries between fact and fiction are impossible to discern. The book is illustrated throughout with photographs, which seem to give credence to the factual basis of the narrative, though the book is called a work of fiction, and the photographs only vaguely correspond to the text. The principal thread is the passage of time: things lost, passed away, diminutively regained and reimagined. The Empress Dowager, the Irish Civil War, a deceased friend, a scale model of the temple of Jerusalem.

Perhaps, in telling his story, Sebald does not participate in it. Perhaps the narrator is Sebald, perhaps not. Perhaps what moves me most about the book is the way in which Sebald is unafraid to take part in his story, to tell only his version of certain events. Perhaps I'm drawn most to detachment. Everything in Sebald's vision finds a relation to everything else, no matter how seemingly distant ideas, objects, people, and memories may be. Disparate voices are all one. Sebald's voice is rare: the voice of a calm mourner, one always accepting of the steady slipping away of everything it can and can't articulate. Sebald seems to be the observer, rather than the writer, of his story. What more could a mourner want than the cool capacity to simply watch without longing? More than the return of all that was lost—that is impossible—the bereaved wish to observe loss happening to them. In life, loss happens too fast to see—it's over before one can know it began; the bereaved want to watch loss defining them.

□

What is a story? Is it different from the narrative made by stringing together a series of memories? Is it the voice of the teller that unifies the story? If I am the author of my story, is this my voice, because it is the voice that speaks the story? To what extent do I choose to take part in the events I am about to recount? Do I choose to tell them, or do I do so because they are all that is available to me and I want to say something, to bring something into being and so define myself? My mother died when I was fourteen; she exists now in the fact of my making. Is my mother a story? Is she, as Sebald says, *A treasure house that existed purely in his head and to which there is no access except through the letters on the page?* Was she always, even before she died?

◻

My mother is alive again. She has returned from death in a hospital, under a doctor's care. We have been told that she is very fragile, that we should expect another death soon. We set her up in the house. Sometimes it is only my father and I. Sometimes my stepmother, stepbrother, and stepsister are there too, caring for my mother, though they did not know her. Sometimes we take her around with us in a car and worry. I am happy. She is alive again, with me. I have longed for her, am always longing. But I know she will be gone again soon and will not come back. I feel a special, precious sadness. I will lose her again, but this time I know I will lose her.

Love is what ties someone to something that goes away. I wake homesick and happy.

◻

Memories lie slumbering within us for months and years, quietly proliferating, until they are woken by some trifle and in some strange way blind us to life. How often this has caused me to feel that my memories, and the labours expended in writing them down are all part of the same humiliating and, at bottom, contemptible business! And yet, what would we be without memory? says Sebald of me and my mother.

I want you to know that I know, and that I am sorry. I was never fair. I asked you from the beginning to believe my story was true. I knew I was changing the facts, or only remembering the ones that would make you feel a certain way. I could not stand for you to feel another way. I could not stand to feel another way myself. *All of us are fantasists, ill-equipped for life, the children as much as myself*, says Sebald. But I know that you knew it was not true, that you always knew, and that you could not bear to tell me, except now and again when you knew it would help me, when you knew you could help me not to be a child anymore.

2

We are staying on Lake George. My father is on our boat. I am in the shallow water with my mother. I am clinging to her body. She is wearing a black swimsuit with a blue V across her chest. She tells me why my father is angry. He wants to take the boat out onto the lake. We do not. She does not like the boat, gets seasick. She reminds me that it is important that we go on the boat, that we show him we enjoy it. I am clinging to my mother, swimming through her legs. I do not want to be separate from her. I like the way the water makes everyone touch everyone else.

I am in my parents' bed, between them. This is what we do on weekend mornings to show our love. My father and I are wrestling, a game of pretend we play. He calls himself "The Phantom." I am a champion wrestler, a hero. My mother cheers me on. I love my father.

My father sat for hours every night beside my mother's bed in the ICU. I know he is a good man. I know he knows something I can only hope to know, can only hope he taught me. What did they do during those hours and days and weeks? She could not talk. In fact, we were never sure whether, during the hours she lived without a liver on the night of her first transplant, she suffered some kind of brain damage. He must have spoken to her, and he must have felt she answered, over the unbearable, wet rhythm of the breathing machine, by gesturing, sometimes scrawling something barely legible on a pad. When he finally divined that she wanted to see me—at first he said she would see no one but him—his evidence was a word painfully scribbled on a yellow sheet of paper. The word resembled my name, if one wanted to see my name there.

▣

For a matter of months when I was nine or ten years old, I could not, or would not, fall asleep in my own bed. I would lie down and my pillow seemed a pool of anxious thoughts. After an hour or so had passed, I would drag my blankets and pillow to my parents' bedroom. At first they resisted, especially my father, but through persistence, I broke them down. I would sleep on their floor, comforted by their alternating snores. The dog curled up beside me. Eventually, I became embarrassed enough by this habit that I resolved to break it. Why did I feel this need to be close to them, to my mother, during the darkest hours? Did I know, though they had never told me, that she was going away? Did I think, if I could hear her restless breathing throughout the night, that I could be sure she would be there in her bed in the morning?

▣

This is what I can remember. The rest is locked away somewhere, to be released, I believe, I hope, when everything is good again. When I realize I am waiting for it, I feel childhood rising within me: powerlessness, hope.

▣

My father's family: his father, an entrepreneur whose businesses, over the course of his life, included gas stations, a sandwich shop called Uncle Milty's, and a trucking company, which upon his early and unexpected death, he left to fail in my father's hands. His mother, a glamorous, beautiful woman about whom I know little, other than that she was funny. My father's sister, an eccentric, a lesbian, a lost child, who, throughout her life, could not hold down a steady job, borrowed, and never repaid, a great deal of money from my father and mother, who also bought her an apartment near our home and sent her to massage school in Gainesville, Florida, though she never subsequently practiced massage. She was by far my favorite and most childlike relative. She and her lover shot themselves together in 1999.

I learned recently that my father's father abandoned the family for several years when my father was a young man. He left and somehow ended up in Hawaii. He had some kind of gambling business, which he taught my father. My grandmother took to drinking.

My father's family had a summer house on Lake George in upstate New York. My father, so he told me, was the 3rd best waterskier on the lake. He supported this claim when, during the many summers my family—my father, my mother, and me—also went to Lake George. One of the happiest times in my childhood must have been the summer he taught me to waterski. I remember my father, otherwise a fairly awkward and clumsy man, gracefully weaving on only one ski across the boat's wake. When he was tired, he would signal to the driver to bring the boat near the beach. My father would let go of the line and glide atop the water on pure momentum, like a duck landing on a still pond.

⊞

I have always kept ducks, he said, even as a child, and the colors of their plumage, in particular the dark green and snow white, seemed to me the only possible answer to the questions that are on my mind, says Sebald.

⊞

We are in the hospital, waiting: my father, my mother's sister, me. I tried to sleep on uncomfortable chairs. It is early in the morning, maybe two or three. Two doctors come through a door, my mother's doctors.

They are walking down the hall, wearing sea-green scrubs. Why are they walking down the hall? The operation is supposed to take fourteen hours. It has only been seven or eight. Can there be early good news? Something has gone wrong. The new liver did not work, did not turn on. She is alive. They are flying in a new liver from somewhere else. It is the wrong blood type but they will put it in for now. I am fourteen years old. She is still alive.

◨

It had been a long and especially hot day, says Sebald, *but FitzGerald remarked on the cool air and remained wrapped tight in his plaid as they drove. At the table he drank a little tea but declined to eat anything. Around nine he asked for a glass of brandy and water and retired upstairs to bed. Early next morning, Crabbe heard him moving about his room, but when he went somewhat later to summon him to breakfast, he found him stretched out on his bed and no longer among the living.*

◨

I was guided to her bed. The ICU was white and terrible. Everyone was connected to machines, tubes worming in and out of them. Beeps and the sound of air being pushed into lungs through tubes by machines. I walked slowly, as if in the dark. My mother had expressed that she wanted her machines disconnected or hidden. I came to her bedside. She had a tube in her throat which forced air into her lungs—a bit of liquid had collected in the tube near her throat; it shook with each thrust of air. Tubes were carrying blood in and out of her. Her skin was yellow and her hair, which had always been dyed blond, was gray. Her hands were thick with fluid. I had brought an essay I had written for class about the book *The Catcher in the Rye*, which I had been reading throughout her hospital stay. I read the essay to her, which I think must have been the cruelest thing I have ever done. She convulsed, as if crying without tears.

3

For a long time I lived on pity. My teachers hardly expected me to complete my schoolwork. The classmates who had made fun of me before no longer did. I do not know what I expected of myself. My guidance counselor took a special interest in me. My father was despondent. We lived alone now in our big house. He and I fought. We took a friend of mine on our annual summer trip to Lake George. This friend told me my father was drunk. I had never known he was drunk, did not know how to recognize it. I could not stop thinking bad thoughts. I began to feel older and older, older than my father, older than my mother had been.

⊡

In my dream, does my mother want to be alive again, or is she alive because she knows I want her to be? Is she scared? She seems to know she will die again soon. She is not scared for herself. She looks at me with a kind of regret, like there is something she hasn't done, will not be able to do. It is not my mother who is fragile.

⊡

You have been willing to help me uphold illusions, live in fantasies. And when you did not, you were better to me, loved me much better, than I was ever willing to say. I fear I have loved you most when you seemed to be going away. You deserve more. The opposite of a story is a promise.

⊡

I have hoped, even, to publish a book-length memoir someday. But the facts would not organize themselves into memories, which are facts told as white lies at best, and the darkest lies at worst. Or this material seemed too boring, or too self-important, or vulnerable to the point of becoming the weakest kind of sentimentality. Poetry seemed too ironic to contain it. Prose too self-serious or without feeling. Determining the order of events seemed impossible. Many are still occurring, or first occurring, right now. Others have yet to take place. *In the final analysis, our entire work is based on nothing but ideas, ideas which change over the years and which time and again cause one to tear down what one had thought to be finished, and begin again from scratch*, he says.

⊡

My poor father.

⊡

My poor mother. My poor stepsister. My poor stepbrother. My poor stepmother. And you, poor, steadfast you, who stood by. You were so good, so giving. You let me believe for so long that I was at the center of my story, when in fact I was telling it, watching from a distance, telling it from far away so that it would happen to you and not me. I made you live my story in my stead. I was not here, with you, where I was needed.

4

My mother hated driving. Her car was an old green Aspen. My father drove a blue Buick. She would only swear when she drove, otherwise she would say "sugar" instead of "shit." She hated changing lanes. She hated using the rearview mirror because she had to take her eyes off the road in front of her. I used to tell her what a good driver she was.

⊡

The two years after my mother died are very hazy, marked in my mind by a few disparate images and an overwhelming sense of grim desolation hanging about our house. Like twin ghosts, my father and I aged beyond our lives and seemed to await the inevitable termination of the present, sharing an aloneness like two prisoners in neighboring cells. If he was not driving me to school, I would often find him still in bed. As I would say goodbye to him, he would say, "I'm staying home from work today. I'm not feeling well." The company that he and my mother had owned together—they were headhunters, finding people jobs in the market research sector—began rapidly failing.

❑

My mother was afraid of dogs, had been bitten by a cocker spaniel as a child. I had begged for a dog. We went to a breeder. I sat in the middle of a bundle of little white puppies. I could pick. I wanted the one that was the friskiest. I named her Frisky. The night we brought her home she went to sleep on the kitchen floor. My father went out to run errands. The puppy must have been very tired. My mother and I were afraid she was sick or dead. We had never had a dog before. My father came home and told us she was fine, just sleeping.

Frisky became my mother's dog. Every morning before she and my father would take me to school and drive to work together, my mother would sit on one of the chairs in the living room. Frisky would come running from another part of the house and leap into my mother's lap. They would stay like that until we left. We had to put Frisky to sleep a few years ago. She was an old dog. She could no longer see or hear and had had a limp.

❑

At some point during my childhood, my father went on an all-liquid diet. For six weeks, he consumed nothing but nutrient shakes, and attended regular monitoring sessions at the office of the company that sponsored the diet. His weight seemed to fall from his body. Years after the diet, when all the weight had come back, my father still kept a picture of himself on the refrigerator, taken shortly after resuming solid food. He wore a tiny bathing suit and looked as thin and young as he ever had.

❑

After my mother died, when he was drunk every night after ten, my father used to slide his feet across the hallway floor and clumsily knock on my door. He would waddle in and collapse on my bed wearing nothing but a pair of underpants and a white T-shirt yellowed at the armpits. He would lecture me about school and, try as I might, I could not dislodge him from my bed. The memory of the sound of his bedroom door opening—which meant he was beginning his nightly round of skulking about the house, binge-eating, and, in his drunken loneliness, berating me with harassing questions—still tightens my guts to this day.

⊡

The first piece of writing I remember being proud of was a paper written in 5th or 6th grade. I no longer remember the topic. What I do remember is my mother standing over me as I typed it out. Perhaps she typed it as I dictated. She told me I was a good writer. I was good at writing. This is what she said I was good at. I did not begin to think of myself as a writer until after her death. I do not think I would have been a writer if she had lived. *Is it not wrong to squander one's chance of happiness in order to indulge a talent?* he asks. Have I done anything she did not tell me to do?

⊡

Perhaps we all lose our sense of reality to the precise degree to which we are engrossed in our own work, and perhaps that is why we see in the increasing complexity of our mental constructs a means for greater understanding, even while intuitively we know we shall never be able to fathom the imponderables that govern our course through life.

⊡

The week before the surgery, the last time she and I could speak, she came home from the hospital. We did not know when the hospital would call but it would be soon. My grandmother—my mother's mother—was staying with us. My mother had been in and out of the hospital for months. We celebrated my fourteenth birthday in a visitor's lounge. She is home, happy. This is the last pure happiness I remember. We walk the dog together up the street. I am still her little boy. I tell her about the new music I like. I have no memory of my father from this week. In fact, I only remember this one day. Not even the day, an hour. Was it even an hour? A minute? Truthfully, I can recall only two images: my mother and grandmother sitting in the living room, my mother standing beside me as we pause on our way up the hill with the dog. I stretched these images into the shape of a week, of happiness.

□

At times on that day, which I recall as being both leaden and unreal, a gap would open up among the billowing clouds. Then the rays of the sun would reach down to the earth, lighting up patches here and there and making a fan-shaped pattern as they descended, of the sort that used to appear in religious pictures symbolizing the presence above us of grace and providence.

□

It has been years since I began writing this piece, and lately I revisited Sebald, reading his last novel, *Austerlitz*. Now it seems clear: Sebald is cold, intellectual, almost unfeeling, except inasmuch as one can feel simply by thinking, or think until feelings are only thoughts and so less potent, less capable of surprise, whether as rapture or despair. What other kind of soul but one ordered by thinking would write *it was only by following the course of time prescribed that we could hasten through the gigantic spaces separating us from each other*? Still, how true that is. But why graft my thoughts about my past onto his? Perhaps he mourns better than I do, and so, in his rambling accounts of one thing yielding to the next, he tells a story that seems real. He understands implicitly—as I would like to understand—that mourning is the means by which a life is lived, in time, in memory, which becomes the present. There is an accrual of power that happens when one understands this—an accrual of calm, which is power in a world that is anything but calm. Telling a story, like reading one, is an act of letting go. *I think how little we can hold in mind, how everything is constantly lapsing into oblivion with every extinguished life, how the world is, as it were, draining itself.* The voice of a story we believe is one that lets things happen, that observes even as it remakes, falsifies, the world by forcing it into words. I read Sebald because I want his voice.

◻

On the night my mother died, I slept next to my father on my mother's side of the bed, where she had last slept months before, where my stepmother would sleep later. I felt nothing. We had driven home from the hospital. It was late. It seemed, that night, like the right thing to do was to remain as close to him as I could. I do not remember that we said anything to each other. I remember lying down in the bed. Then I must have slept. He must have too. I must have awoken in the morning. The world must have been changed. We must have stood up. We must have gone about our lives. It must have been years since then.

PART THREE

To an Editor Who Said I Repeat Myself
and Tell Too Much

The mouth works all its life to spit a vowel—
some long sound with feeling fenced in
by the sharp stops of a few consonants, a howl
and a pen to keep it tame, a calm din
that won't drown out the life it tries
to say, but won't deny, either, that hell
is the sound we're born making, the cry
in the womb, which we tell
and tell—too much, of course—
in the hope of exhausting it. Stated plain,
there is no other subject—rejoice, remorse,
repress—all words stand for pain.
Over and over I say—what else can I do?
All words stand for pain. Fuck you.

Get Out

Can you feel your confidence
match the billowing crowd?
You even feel cocky, believing

you've earned the admiration of a few.
It is, in fact, what it appears to be:
a voice fastened to paper very carefully,

a cry cut from its mouth.
But then, you think, who is that
you're talking to? There's no one here,

just paper and ink and you.
What is this pathetic game
of pretend? Get out. Go find a friend.

"Sometimes We Sleep Well in the Midst of Terrible Grief"

The January night my mother died
the bed was wet and heavy with snow.
Things felt mostly odd, and no one cried.

We stared blank as graves dug from inside
as my dad and I drove home straight and slow
the January night my mother died.

Her death was like waking up to fried
food cooking on another family's stove
in another life where no one cried,

because no one had known her, or they denied
having known her their whole
lives the morning after my mother died

in a hospital where a social worker tried
to prepare us to let the bleeping machines go
silent, nothing to measure. No one cried

and I slept by my dad on my mother's side
of their bed. I wanted to know,
on the January night my mother died,

how she had slept. A few years later, I cried.

My Mom, d. 1994

My wife is not my mom. My mom is not
my mom. My father is not my mom. My boss
is not my mom. She is a tooth with rot,
a flower pressed between the pages of a lost
book. My son is not my mom. She is a mare
crushing my skull beneath her hoof. She is forever
starved. I ride to the edge of the earth clutching her hair.
Get it over with. It's never OK, not ever.
Fuck it, whatever. If Robert Frost is my mom,
then so is Robert Lowell. She taught me to talk.
She is where I'm headed, a bomb
crater. She forgives me like a hunting hawk.
Maybe she's my boss's boss, my wife's other other lover,
my son's midnight cough. She loves me like a brother.

Quatrains Until Dawn

Well here we are. Does night
race or erase the time
between now and morning?
This voice makes my brain sick.

It's heard it all before
and that's it. Well death is
just like anything else.
Check the clock. Whole years can

fit between tick and tock.
Race or erase the time
tonight, its long private
fever, its terrible blank,

real as any audible voice.
Well here we are halfway.
Hold this in your hand and
feel this. Who would take

care of my wife and son?
Well there it is.
Worries not razor blades.
They are just plain dull.

Well soon the sun will be up.
If only my headphones
can sing me to sleep. Well
soon the sun will be up.

PART FOUR

I

Goodbye Girls

It's time to stop clutching
you last few petals, dreams
I've been sleeping without. So

goodbye dear missed Marisa
and Cath and Debra
and Tanya and dearest Renee—

I leave you for the life
you left me to, but, still, I pine
for you and all the men

I might have become
between your various kisses
(if only I had kissed you enough

or at all, lips soft and warm as
possibilities). Now look at you
on Facebook, your children hoisted

upon your hips, their faces only half-
familiar. I read your debut articles
in *The Nation*, browse pics of Brazil

and your living rooms. You're so
much better than we would have
been. I hope there is nothing

like me (did you even *like* me?)
in the men you chose,
who got you for their wives,

leaving no reason for their thoughts
to circle back to bygone girls
with whom they didn't get to live

other, better lives.

Late Poem

I was alone inside a book as I'd wished. It was
fifty years from now. I didn't live that long.
The book was lost, in an attic, a locked trunk,
a storage space, under rubble. It was the last
copy, the only. Immortality seemed a memory.
My journals were lost or incinerated, those fervent
transcriptions and wonderings and hopeful
evenings, scripts for wild lives unlived, unloved
long since disintegrated. Whatever power
I encoded had escaped and moved on. I was
neither I nor eye nor lie. No one cared or could.
Even what was left of me wasn't. My bones
were as brittle as a text, religious, with no teacher.
Looking back, there was no future, no future.

Narcissus and Me

*A reflection is irresistible because it is a paradox:
an opposite that is the same, an other that is also
clearly yourself.*

—Daniel Mendelsohn

If they weren't mine, I'd say
my eyes are beautiful,

like a riddle
to which I am the answer.

I'd say my eyes are green,
flecked with orange—women

have always admired my eyes.

◻

My beard is a blazing
red, I'd say.
          Some women admire it.

Even, perhaps, some men.

◻

*A vision overwhelmed him—
an empty hope,
          a shadow mistaken for it's body.*

*He gazed at himself, wonderstruck
and paralyzed.
          He saw his own two eyes*

like two green stars,
his beard divinely curling.

It was desire for himself
that seized him,
                    longing

to know the one closest to hand, farthest from reach.

⊡

I would say my eyes
are a woman's eyes.

Even my beard, I'd say,
should grow on the face
                    of a woman.

Green is the color of springtime
and birth—
                    mine are the eyes

of a woman's feelings.

And red is also a woman's color,
like flowers and sex.

But my shoulders are broad
as a wall,
                    my gut as tough as a rock.

⊡

Only a thin, thin line keeps us apart,
more forbidding than mountains

or impassable gates.

I would ask,
what kind of man
                    has eyes so green?

I would look into my eyes
and ask to love.

But they are my eyes
and there are things I do not know

how to ask.

◨

I am the cause
                    of the fire,

the fuel and the flame
it feeds.

Smoking

I smoke a pipe—it's ridiculous, I know, I know.
One of those silly habits taken up in high school
—to seem older? Different? Certainly not cool—
and accidentally kept up as the years go.
What do I think this is, the nineteenth century
when all young men smoked pipes? I'm thirty,
a father, overweight, and smoke *two hours a day*!
My son, who'll need care, can't afford my dying young
of throat-rot or cancer of the tongue.
The trouble is I *like* it. I read Sherlock Holmes—
a pipe's the right accessory for thinking, writing poems.
And maybe I still feel older than I am, still feel
different, mistreated, odd, and want to repay
my past's pain with future pain, a smoker's deal.

Friendship

In just the couple years since two by two
we all began to partner off,
already we've practically retired, passing through
apartment doors shut tighter than a cough.
There used to be long, wasted hours of talk,
nothing secret between us, not even skin;
at the conclusion of a wandering walk,
the flirtatious dark would set in.
Is marriage lonely by design,
in hopes that obeying an age-old law
of *I am only hers, she is only mine*
forms a brittle scab over the always-raw
wound of too much intimacy between friends
in favor of a duller aching that never ends?

Other Women

There are other women everywhere,
long legs pouring into sandals, feet almost bare,
shampoo-floral-odor tail trailing
like the tail of a comet that comes hailing
every fifteen seconds, spanning one generation
at most of skittery male temptation.
I touch them all in quick succession, their thighs
and each plump buttock fondled by my eyes.
If they knew, if they knew—oh but they must:
men and women are bound by public lust.
Every turn of my head is a secret tryst
I rehash while fucking my wife, and I'm not missed
at home in bed. How lovely, all this sex in the air—
wherever I look, a blameless affair!

Masturbation

Painstakingly, thoroughly, you do in your head what you'd never do
        in life,
every lick and thrust and slap, every delicious source of shame,
all these desires—*real desires*—you would never tell your wife
or anyone, though she, who wishes you'd talk dirtier, wouldn't blame
you for being turned on by anything. But you believe—you always
        have—
there's something sick about the thoughts that get you off, your
        personality
damaged, a hurt somewhere that might hurt someone you love.
Ironic—or not?—that what shames you most is most organically
yourself. It will erupt, you fear, and possess you, this demon from
        your core,
where you are always terrified alone and your traumas are fossilized.
For years you did it once a day, at least, if not two or three times
        more,
out of boredom, or to mellow after a glance at a classmates's inner
        thighs.
But not lately. Now it's once or twice a month, far less than you have
        sex for real.
You're a good person, you don't do anything wrong, no matter what
        you feel.

Jazz

It's not the idea of collective improvisation I like,
not the show of instrumental virtuosity,
not the hipster life. And jazz isn't my history.
No, when the tune is really going, when horns spike,
dip into and slice the melody, when the drums
kick the rhythm deep and the bass is walking
and you hear the wooden click before the E-string thrums,
I love that, without any words, these people are talking
like they can say exactly what they mean
because they never have to say it.
Rather than labor to construct a sentence, they play it.
How fun! O, to play the piano, to let my thoughts careen
instead of getting stalled in speech. Talking takes so long
and never helps. I wish Brenda and I could fight in song.

The Middle Generation

They rewrote their lives, ahead of and obsessed with themselves.
Their books seem to tremble a little, unsettling my shelves.

They did nothing good, except for their art, if art meant
pillorying their loved ones in poems, setting the precedent

for so much sentimental verse in the ensuing decades,
pathetic, melodramatic poems as dull as used razor blades.

They were jealous and fake, and drank with inspired, suicidal thirst,
but if I could write poems like their best, I'd forgive me at my worst.

Of course, now dead and all but mythic, they can be anything
I need them to, and I can be like them, so in my reimagining,

they wrote blindly past the point of retreat, and they are, like me,
choked swans sinking slow and graceful into the black of posterity.

Money Time

Supposedly, time is money:
money will buy you time
assuming you have money

to spend, as well as time
to wait while your money
grows. However, time

spent waiting can be like money
misspent—it's often time
wasted, even if money

is made, a kind of time
not worth spending, so money
isn't necessarily time.

Maybe time is money
if you make with your time
something else that makes money,

though most of the time
it's not *your* money
you've made with your time.

And money isn't even money,
necessarily, in a time
like this, when money

loses value and time
is misspent losing money.
And time isn't even time,

necessarily, if it's lost money
on which you're wasting time,
nor is money really money

if it's wasted on wasted time.
Still, sometimes, time *is* money,
but only if you have money and time.

Layoff

In my twenty-ninth year, and in the two
thousand and ninth since the birth of Christ,
I was laid off from my job. I worked
as a book reviews editor and news
reporter for the major industry
magazine of the publishing business.
Hardly anyone advertises now,
certainly not to other businesses,
so I was let go. I can't take it
too personally—who isn't being laid off
these days? I get more time with my young son,
can freelance, teach poetry, write about books,
plus there's unemployment for now and work
as a secretary for an old artist friend.
And my wife is still working; we're OK.
But, still, I have more time, the very thing
I took a nine-to-five job to get rid of, and time
brings things to mind: how's and why's and what's
that make the day like a sleepless night.
What did I do wrong? And how will I get
healthcare for my son once my severance is done?
My brain spilleth over and gets on everyone.

⊡

Cal has just gone to sleep. It's eight o'clock,
Sunday night, and tomorrow might as well
be Saturday. Lately Cal's been resisting
bed, crying for hours till he just can't anymore
and begins to quietly snore, as if sleep
were one more submission forced upon him.
Or is that an adult's idea? An adult sprung
suddenly free—he just wants this not that,
like me, and sleep is that for now.

What's to be gleaned from what a child
does and why? He's simply not given to
interpretation, mine or his own. That's
the lesson: some things aren't anything
else. Then, later, all things are other things,
their meanings trumping how they be.
A day job affords distraction
from this kind of ruminating. What Auden said
about poetry, that it makes nothing happen,
is also true of thinking, though what good
does that thought do? Tomorrow,
how will the impossible problems
of each succeeding moment make any more sense
than they do today? What will my son become
and what can I do for or about it now?
I'm being vague, I know, but that's part
of the problem, isn't it—not saying
what I won't know I think till it's said. How
do I learn to love Brenda right, and learn
to get her to love me how I want to be loved?
What's love look like in the midst of a fight?
Where does being good meet being right?
I won't linger on my hardest feelings.
Line them in silver, turn them downside up—
so I can say I'm OK all the time. What does it
feel like to linger on a feeling? Stand patiently
in mud and suffer its stink and suck.
Know thyself by thine unwashed smell, thine crust.
I need to be good, that's how my mother
made me, but she's dead and I'm grown
and you can't be a man and be good all the time.
At work, someone would have come by to ask
my help by now with a dumb, blessèd task.

□

I'm looking at a reproduction
of a painting by Dorothea Tanning
of a lapdog, man-size, dancing
with a corpselike naked woman. The dog turns
his face toward the viewer, serious gaze,
judging eyes, adorable jowls, paws.
Something about this picture makes me think
anything is possible, and reminds me
most things aren't. Those who can bear the grim
facts of their lives, face them without recasting
them in rosier terms, impress me. I talk
a lot about my choices, facing my share
of bad turns, but I ride on a gloss
of sunshine. I love phrases like "all shall
be well and all manner of thing shall be well,"
as if the irony they clearly belie
were a figment of a cynic's inner grimace.
For four years now I've been
taking an antidepression, anti-
anxiety drug, and I'll never know
to what extent my capacity to sometimes
clean my mental slate, to move away
from worries—that's what it feels like now, I can
move on, pass by, think about something
else—I owe to the drug, and what's due to
therapy and trying hard at my life.
I don't want to be so mad at my wife.

□

Listening to an online stream of an album
by Richard Buckner, his plain, almost flat
voice and lush arrangements. I like
unmusical elements in music—
with a voice like his, he shouldn't sing,
but he does and so aspires
to, and attains, beauty and other

wordless quirks, making it more
than organized sound. I like the unpoetic stuff
that crops up in poetry too: casual speech
amidst sonorous language, ugly words,
avoidance of the transcendent. The un-
beautiful in both mediums points to
the notion that art is at least fifty
percent choice, that beauty is indeed
in cahoots with its beholder and maker,
just as the mirror can only reflect
the one who chooses to stand before it.
Most of this poem comes straight
from my life, a record of events set
in rhythmic words. But life's unpoetic,
and how will Brenda be hurt, and Cal,
by being my excuse to dredge my brain?
Did Lowell's loved ones ever get over
For Lizzie and Harriet? Plath's son
just killed himself. As I check my
Twitter feed for mentions of an article
I wrote that came out today,
my son gets speech and feeding therapy
while Brenda watches and I sit in my
home office living my online life. Real life,
not Auden's stale suffering and "its
human position," is a bunch of things
that don't add up to much, happening
at the same time, a series of tries.
"Beauty is truth, truth beauty," but isn't life
as it is beautiful and full of lies,
and life as written true and made to revise?

◫

Brenda brought home a coatrack from Ikea.
Of course, it comes in a flat brown box
full of rods and hooks and screws, assembly

required, and, of course, I dropped the small
middle rod into the bottom one—got it stuck—
while we were giggling and putting it
together, and an explosion followed.
I have so little patience for her
temper, how it beckons mine from
nearby where it waits to pounce.
I shouldn't blame her, though. There's not nearly
enough—of what? some basic energy?—
to go around, to share, to sustain us two
and Cal and a house and the work we do.
I'm afraid of what will happen when
too much of this anger starts to accrue.
But aren't anger and resentment two of
the things a marriage is meant to contain,
that couples take to graves, that bloom after rain?

For a living I still write about books, and
recently, I profiled the author of a novel
called *You or Someone Like You*—it comes out
next month—in which the heroine, named Anne
Rosenbaum, can only communicate
with her husband, a Hollywood exec
named Harold, who is pulling away,
through these book clubs she runs for film bigwigs
who gossip her pronouncements on love
and literature back to Harold, who
finally comes around. I will show this
poem to Brenda before anyone else,
and I can't help but think I want her
to take its implicit apologies
seriously, store them, a first-aid kit
against all that makes our love delicate.

Everything now depends on progression,
or, as the truth may be, pretends to it.
Being laid off thwarts or spurs progress, but
Cal must learn new ways to compensate for
what his injury took, and we,
Brenda and I, must talk more and listen
better. All of it gets measured
on a continuum plotted between
imaginary points placed at the worst
we were, or imagine we were, and now
—the worst and best we are—and as good
as we'll get before time's up, our losses cut
and our gains written down in The Big Book
no one gets to read. Do people progress?
Can I change? If so, how would I know? I guess
happiness is the benchmark, the vague way
it has of being remembered, as if
the past was always better or worse
than now, rather than the same. It makes me ache
for my favorite line by Frost, from "Directive":
"Drink and be whole again beyond confusion,"
he says, the happiest of fantasies,
as if we were whole once, or aren't now
but could be again, no longer confused—
can anyone reach that far point before being dead,
relax, stretch out, hum, read, just bask,
and not regret what was and wasn't said?

□

What I liked best about work was structure,
a place to go where I knew I should be,
the sense that my time had already been bought,
that to use it for myself broke a rule—
I like rules, was raised by them, doing a dance
with my mother whose steps involved committing
minor sins she didn't like, bowing with guilt,

apologizing till I wore her down,
then doing it all again and again.
It's cheap, I know, to blame her, but fair.
She died, as my poems say, just before
I could grow up and out of childhood,
and so I never really do. I've looked
for her everywhere since and found her most
when I could recreate our sad ballet:
easy enough occasions to find: marriage, job,
anywhere anyone, especially
a woman, expects anything of me.
The world is overripe with surrogate moms,
it turns out, and I'm a willing son. It's
pathetic. I'm a child wrapped in the life
of a man. Of course, who isn't?
Understanding has just so much to give.
Psychology can take us only so far.
To go the rest of the way we have to—what?
Wait? hope? forget? forgive? talk? just live?

◫

It's a funny word, layoff, what I wish
everyone, everything would do more of:
lay off me, give me a break, let me be:
less pressure, fewer appointments, less need,
not so much to worry about, no more
doctor's visits and therapy sessions
for Cal, no more books for me to read,
no arguments to have, no dishes to do, no more
blame to assign, no more Even
Stevens, and no more syllabi to write,
no more student poems to comment on,
no more diapers to change, no more sleep lost,
no more hours passed, no more compromises,
no more messages to check, no more e-mails
to which to reply, no more self-states

to navigate and synthesize, no more
about myself I didn't know till now,
no more coatracks to assemble, no more
hopes I should have already outgrown,
no more incomplete mourning to trick me
into feeling like someone's not dead,
no more anxiety attacks or fear of
fear itself, no more Paxils chopped in two,
no more endless nights or sleep without rest,
no more dreams about building towers
of colored blocks on islands that float away
too soon, no more dead dogs to mourn,
no more fathers blamed, no more mothers lost,
no more in-laws, mine or yours, no more step-
sisters or brothers whose Evites need answers,
no more lost ways or ways nearly found,
no more mp3s to crave, no more wavy
red lines hashed by spellcheck, no more friends'
manuscripts to exchange, no more blog posts,
no more teaching opportunities, no more
nights facing your back or you facing mine,
no more free time, no more busy days,
no more beers or bottles of wine, no more
30 Rock on Thursday nights, just some space
and time that no one needs, some extra air,
new names, a face no one could recognize,
a small world, a view exactly the size of my eyes.

◫

How can I propose to write a poem
about being laid off during the Great Recession
and avoid money, which, if it doesn't
make the world go round, can surely stop it
from chilling out, which, after all, may
well be the real reason man was put on earth.
Give me an eternity of ease,

he seems to say, and I'll suffer whatever
you throw my way in the lifetime before
forever starts, though don't expect me
not to complain. I'm speaking in generalities
rather than talk about money and Brenda
and me. For a couple of years now,
she's made much more than I have, teaching
and working from home and taking care of Cal.
I was out of the house most of the time
at my nine-to-fiver, not making much
more than I spent, often less, but bringing
steady checks and health insurance.
No end of argument ensued about who
provided what, on whose shoulders burdens
belonged. Neither of us knows what counts
for more once it's thrown into the family cup.
How like a company is a family?
Is money its reason and its root,
what brings it together, breaks it apart?
Harder to say with families who's in charge,
but to keep love going the cost is large.

⊡

Keats calls for Negative Capability:
"when a man is capable of being
in uncertainties, Mysteries, doubts without
any irritable reaching after fact
and reason." If only he meant
being capable while being negative,
a useful quality, too, I suppose. He means,
of course, imagining against the backdrop
of reality and all the ways it opposes
our little dreams, this business
of truth and beauty being the same.
But could a man who died childless
at twenty-six have known much about how ugly

truth can be, how far toward good
lies can carry us? Very far, I've learned,
though a time for reckoning always comes,
many times for many lies, and, I think,
we go on that way, leaping from hope
to hope across the ample evidence
that what we hope can't come to pass.
Life is off the page, and bearing
down, being here, means being in one
place right now, much harder, it seems,
than being in two—our bed, my thoughts.
The days are so far from ideal, but
the ideal is merely a thought away
from anywhere, anywhen. How to pick
now, this, us, as it is, when there's
so much else right here in my head?
I'm not very brave. I would be much
braver could I wake and not need to say
—I don't think I can—it will be OK.

□

I've got too much thought and nowhere
to think it. I need to stop, to move on,
to choose, to act, to lay off myself and you.
If poetry and thinking both do nothing
then the longer I write the less I choose
to do. Is that what I want, who I hope
to be, someone who sits before a scrawling page,
a ream, if you will, as thick as the sky
is deep, with room enough for all the words
but for none of what they signify?
I said what matters is who I address
and how and why, not what is said,
but, really, if I'm to make anything
of this column I've spun like a droning
A/C, which cools the room while it's on

then invites the sweat back in, what matters
is *that* I address—and not in poetry,
which maybe lasts forever, but, as Auden said,
only "survives in the valley of its making,"
a place, I fear, with a peerless, immortal view,
but merely a mirage in our actual lives—
what matters, all that matters, is *that* I say
something, anything, aloud to Brenda.
We fight not to say what we can't or won't,
to say anything but what we know we need
to hear. I'm sorry, Brenda, I haven't been
listening—I've hardly been awake, avidly
drilling down toward an imaginary center.
How selfish to go on like this for pages
without even a pause for a word, an inkling
from you. Tell me, what are you thinking?

Lines in the Rain

You, dear Brenda, are at home
with our son, whose remarkable
days have him laughing
like any kid he isn't. When
we made him out of the wish

to make him, we knew nothing
except our own parents couldn't be
close or far enough.
Our son can't run, which may
be our fault, we'll never know,

like sitting on separate daggers.
Love is the need to escape
the beloved, isn't it? So you can
pretend you can't cause any pain?
It's a mutation of guilt, isn't it?

I hide beneath sheets, close
to your belly, and apologize
—to you, to my mother, to our son,
to motherhood and fatherhood,
to all those now fleeing

what they love. It's grotesque,
but I will cough something up,
a bloody string of self, to tie
you to me, me to him, him to you,
then we can all go our ways,

separate or not, or nowhere, and pluck
that string, feel each other
tensing, teasing the other end.

You may not understand—I don't
either—but someday we might:

Someday shines on families like light.

II

The Meantime

It's easy to overjoy a window with brilliant flowers
but what if long-longed-for time suddenly bubbled
over the lip of the clock, as if each day doubled
due to a lost job or loved one slaughtered, leaving hours
to fill—how would you do it? Could you whittle
the Founding Fathers faces out of wood, or fold little
origami models of the same famous building?
With time, couldn't you master the craft of anything?
Maybe write precious verse or, worse, illuminate
the best of Aesop in needlepoint—someone ought to,
or maybe someone really oughtn't, so why, or why not you?
If time's a parking spot, life's what you do while you wait
for Mr. Whoever to get back in the car—a good hobby
to make this minute count like a droplet in the sea.

The Darkness Echoing

Any improper collection or misuse of information
provided on Facebook is a violation of the Facebook
Terms of Service and should be reported...
—Facebook Privacy Policy

Blames his father. Lost his job. Can't escape
this sentence. Has and has not become
what he most despised. Never saw or sees
shapes in clouds. Has grown accustomed

to autocorrect. Wants to be interesting,
mostly to himself. Types this on his iPad.
Wonders if that counts as aphorism and
whether he still has what he once had.

Is impressed with how promises of sadness
are so often fulfilled. Wishes he could push restart.
Understates. Is accustomed to therapy.
Plans to pull his inner and outer lives apart.

Hopes online is where love becomes clear.
Doesn't know his friends. Cannot make it cohere.
Just got cable. Is unable to state his decision.
Feels like a knife balancing on its own incision.

Home

You leave your emotions all over the apartment
like the empty glasses you leave all over
the apartment, wine rings at the bottom, dregs
I mostly fail to scrub out. I feel you
seething under every paper towel, starched
and stained with coffee and applesauce.
I pick them off tables like a quiet maid.
You know I shiver at the mess, left in trade
for the piles of my books left blocking,
then killing your thirsty plant, for the dishes
piled high in the sink until you can't
rinse your hands or find a fork. You spread
your books across my side of the bed.
While you sleep I press my foot against your leg.

Fame

I sleep like a rock usually, snoring like a rock grinder.
Mostly it's Brenda who can't fall asleep—any reminder
of tomorrow's work, or today's, makes her thoughts spin.
When I'm worried awake, it's mostly about dying, or Cal, alone—
who will take care of him when Brenda and I are dead?
But sometimes I like to think of my writing with sweet pity.
It's a delicious hurt, this kind of self-indulgent drone
in which two of tomorrow's readers remember me:
"He was a prolific small press poet, good, not great.
His wife was a major writer. I think I used to own, or read,
one of his books—it was sarcastic, grumpy, and grim.
A *very* minor Robert Lowell, with a dash of James Tate,"
is what I imagine they'll say when they look back,
"and he died sometime in the 2030s of a heart attack."

The Past Ahead

I find myself looking forward to the past,
confident remembering will lengthen it,
that even forgetting will make it last

a little longer, as all the amassed
memory returns in flashes bit by bit.
It seems so accessible, so near, the past,

as though it were my own very vast
place, neither behind nor ahead, easy to visit.
The *fact* that it doesn't last

makes no sense. I hardly have to cast
thoughts backward before I inhabit
—so why not look forward to?—the past,

full of real things I can pick up—the glass
dancer my mother loved, the statuette
my father bought her for their last

anniversary, the anniversary of which just passed.
She's dead; that's all that caused their split.
She's all I'd go back for; otherwise the past

is forgettable at last. The dead last.

Like an Answer, Yes

Death will come like a cool glass of water,
like one among the countless leaves you see,
like a car, any car, driven by a son or daughter,

and like an answer, yes, but there are so many
for each question, and, anyway, the right one
is only right when it happens to be.

It will come in a last breath, or just after breath is gone,
or just before a first breath, or one squarely
in between, a deep breath, say, along your daily run.

It will come like a wish fulfilled, a wish barely
made, which, once granted, is always
different than what you wished. Be safe; wish warily.

It will come like money, which usually pays
the same—there's always less and always more.
It will come like a messenger from yesterday,

who, though you can't enter, holds open a door,
or, even before you bring her home, your new wife,
who is already carefully keeping score.

But it's not death that scares you. It's the rest of your life.

BOOK TWO: A CELEBRATION

Beginnings for an Essay in Spite of Itself

I can't precisely say how but I always knew, for instance, I might. Yet in my dream he was standing and dirty playing in the dirt while those of us on the committee drank and deliberated and our dear one took care distractedly. I have to go somewhere in a car. And so it begins. Or so it begun, and it goes on.

⊞

I'm thinking of something. It almost starts as a finished product, loose, changing (kind of like how Saul Bellow used to phone Ringo Starr all hours of the night), so things won't feel out of place or, worse, rejected. It might be what goes on in that head of his.

⊞

Because ninety-nine percent of secrets are kept by accident, those revealed on television let alone social media account for less than the way the sun is so small. It can't be seen from another vantage point in the universe, should anyone attain such a perspective alone. The phone rings, but I wouldn't have wanted to answer it.

⊞

I don't believe any of that about the self in the world being parceled out, not really being the self, and I have no faith whatsoever that the "I" in one sentence bears any relation to the "I" in the next. The reader could close his or her eyes and reopen them on someone else's prose.

⊞

Ever in the midst of a fashion show, the heart is concerned about career. The part of you that was laughing at you is still laughing at you though now another part, not the one the first part was laughing at, but another that was watching for a while, is laughing at the laughing part.

□

The most painful are the things you would do most tenderly. An ending isn't a cure for anything, yet, as a child, I believed myself fated for greatness or luck so dismal it could be a kind of greatness. But I would still have had to make all these choices, which is why all poetry has been suspended.

□

The earth and moon will fall out of orbit if either closes its eye. So it is with the two of us. I want to have the nature of an essay—a hypothesis, proofs, a conclusion—crossed with that of a confession (here is what I did and why; I regret but would not have done otherwise)—but the various sentences should ignore each other, have ends that simply won't knit together. Perhaps in the middle the piece could mention itself as a clue.

□

But is it truly suffering if you survive, are remade, even enhanced? Is suffering an upgrade, a walkway toward booby-trapped tune-ups? Whoever answers gets $3,000 from the Administration for the Preservation.

□

Bragging rights to him who suffers most, to him who suffers most dramatically. The performance of suffering is a social contract between person and pain and fans taking notes against the dawning of their own pain, like the day a ship first leaves port marked with a soldier's beautiful scar.

□

A nest of flowers: what made it? A bird?

□

If only I could start to speak from his vantage point rather than my own, to know what he does, to be one of them, lucky few. Every night for an hour in his bed crying like a staple in his foot like he wants to spit up blood before finally letting himself fall.

⊡

He was so tired, speaking of the luck when a lion crosses your path.

⊡

Life is not an antidote to itself. That's how plaque was discovered between most library books. Snow fell, denoting a required field. You have mixed feelings aboard the train speeding from love to love, where you can sense me grinding.

⊡

Thank you for grinding. You could be so sad if only you'd try. She who looked upon you would weep. She who touched you would grow cold. She who talked with you hours into the night would tomorrow find only water where her ears had been. She who promised her life to you would have all the tears she wanted and good company beside every deathbed.

⊡

I wanted my story sideways, without asking anything of anyone or presuming I felt anything anyone else couldn't. I wanted, finally, to author a story that wasn't mine in particular, but belonged to me and anyone who read it, a story no one would be jealous of or shun, a story no one would ask questions about nor be able to anticipate, a spontaneous story as old as a fable, a story someone could give back to me as a gift. I'd be so grateful.

Grief: A Celebration

Heaven must be dying on time
at the end of a long life, family
at hand, goodbyes hovering

like hummingbirds, which,
if one is absolutely still,
sometimes land on a finger and sip

honey as if from nowhere. One would feel
full as at the end of a rare meal
prepared by an old friend, for which

one has brought a dessert to say
thanks. Whatever one feared,
it did not come to pass, as it never

does, at least not quite
as one feared. There is nothing
to regret because all has been

forgiven, and, anyway, this was
a trial run. And so, when
a newly-minted angel

of death comes to the door—she has just
earned her wings, her flight
was unsteady—your family offers

a drink and a seat at the table, which,
of course, she politely declines,
before you joyfully take her hand,

walking backwards toward the exit,
both of you blowing kisses and
laughing like newlyweds boarding a cruise.

The distance between us is
actually composed of time
more than space, though there is space

between us, too, but it's not
as important. Celebration
can be a kind of grieving, an aspect of grief

and vice versa, which is to say
grief is not necessarily sad. I'm lucky
to have had these few loved ones

die on me, and these few others
live on as though dying, on the
very edge of death, an impurity

that nonetheless cleanses, like
the subtext of a very long,
meandering sentence trailing off.

Adulthood came early,
swooping like a hungry owl, beautiful
and dangerous. That

is what I wish someone would offer:
absolution. Great responsibility
overcame me, an illness, a revelation

as when in *Swann's Way* little Marcel
is absolved, his "unhappiness . . . regarded
no longer as a punishable offense

but as an involuntary ailment which had been
officially recognized." Is a few more
hours of childhood so much to ask? No,

but it is far too much to grant.
And who might one ask, anyway,
without annoying them?

The children everyone loves seem to know
the answers already; they ask
the questions just to be polite.

◫

Nobody knows at the beginning.
Only gradually, as the beginning
begins to end, and then after it's over,

but before the very end, does the self
reveal to the self what the self
has always known.

There are some things you don't
write down, not secrets, just facts
beneath the necessity of articulation,

of a minor frequency, a local broadcast
in the beat-up, way-out town
in your heart, where some uncles live

without wives or other serious ties
to women. These are things you know
to be true, which would be truer

if you found words for them,
as if they were discovered by someone else
who told the whole school before

you got there one fateful morning.
Don't pretend there isn't a high school
in you you just can't graduate:

you're not popular there, but at least
everyone knows who you are.
It's one place you'll always belong.

□

Another one about trying to grasp
time, to grip it like a rough rope
sliding through blistering hands,

in which each of his chances
scuttles beyond him, in which he
imagines that through description, naming,

he might make more of his time.
Let's get to work, try and calm down.
Let's be nice for a change. Who are we?

It's the two of us—you and me—or just
myself and another self, also mine,
but less so, like a little cousin,

a drop without a pool to join.
Is it strange that I sometimes feel
like an intruder in someone else's home town,

despite, or because of, having been invited?
The mind is a little party where one stands
in the corner and waits

for a fantasy girl to stroll up
and coax one into conversation. Of course
she won't, so one is merely waiting

for an appropriate chance to leave.
As soon as one such occasion
disappears, another comes into focus.

What would it feel like to live
forever? Would you forget sometimes
and assume your death was inevitable,

that this might be your last taste,
only to be struck dumb, suddenly robbed
of your appetite, when you recall

that you have more time ahead of you
than the gods, who will die
just before you do, when the last atom

of your faith expires, O old one.
Even the gods have their doubts.
Even they can't scratch every itch.

If you could feel no pain, wouldn't you
long for it, try and try to hurt yourself
just for a change? Even the gods need a break.

And there's description: as if
to get into words, and therefore into
the mind, what the eyes

or the ears or the fingers detect
could keep the fleeting world
from fleeing. Who hasn't

chosen a particularly delicious
memory over, say, a tedious half hour
while a band plays and everyone

is watching them, no one watching you?
You're free to think? Words are souvenirs.
If I could be anywhere now, wouldn't I?

Not because I would make different
choices, but because it pains me
to think that I now no longer

have the option to have made
different choices. Which is another way of saying
no matter what we did we would end up

at the end of the long hallway without
doors or turns, just a straight,
inevitable passage, like a bad idea.

Nothing feels right. Feelings
are like someone else's clothes.
Nonetheless you might be identified.

I make lists when I'm most afraid,
as though, if I just keep at it,
I will finally get home to where

my mother and me are how we were.
Life is as fragile as a sheet of bible paper.
There is only one world, and no one makes it

all the way there. I say things like that
to myself to explain everything I love,
which is trending toward decay.

□

You are always preparing, preparing,
and then nothing happens,
an eventuality for which you were unprepared.

At the very core of fear is the obvious,
too deep to see and too simple to understand—
professionals have died trying, their bones

lining the path that leads
to the answer, which is complex
but also the same text as the one

inscribed on a plaque by the entrance.
I have yet to meet anyone so different
from anyone else I've met. I even recognize

myself reflected in the puddles of others'
mistakes. Did you ever notice how
they pool, making rainbows?

◫

Upon first publication, each page
is like a temple along the pilgrimage
to that most holy shrine, The End.

And so I took the easy way, if only
because I was surprised I found it.
I've been tempted since to try the hard way,

just to compare or to have something to say
to the next in line. But there are some steps
you can't retrace, because something

swept over the footprints behind
or I really wasn't paying attention. It seems
—doesn't it?—like the whole world is erased.

There really is no distinction
between worship and superstition.
The heavens are wide enough to hold

everyone's cries, but too wide
for anyone to hear them. You have
the very pervasive sense that if you just

keep talking you'll make it,
though embarrassment is only a symptom
of what truly unsaddles you.

You are almost across the covered bridge.
Once on the other side, though, you'll see
another bridge, this one uncovered.

⊡

The snake swallows its tail despite the taste.
You imagine yourself old amongst trophies:
the thick volume of collected works,

dozens of toothy children beaming
out of wooden frames, grounds
stretching in all directions.

And then follows the thought that none of it
can prevent death from strolling
right through the door (no matter how

it's barred) and then leaving with
what it came for. Heaven must be
smiling on your deathbed as your soul

seeps upward, vaporizing.
Perhaps it's better to die behind
one's own back. Those who know

are never available. Yet each death feels
so exceptional, as if, simply due to the odds,
some people ought to be spared.

Is there truly time for so many tragedies?
Death has earned the key to every city. For who else
tends to all of the sick? Who else takes

in the old? Who else wants us all?
Not even our mothers. In fact,
only death always keeps its promise.

Notes

"Sometimes We Sleep Well in the Midst of Terrible Grief" takes its title from a line in "Submission to Death" from James L. White's *The Salt Ecstasies*.

"On His Bed and No Longer Among the Living": The italicized passages and title are taken from W. G. Sebald's books *The Rings of Saturn* and *Austerlitz*.

"Narcissus and Me": The italicized passages are my versions, with serious liberties taken, of passages from the "Echo and Narcissus" section of Ovid's *Metamorphoses*.

"The Darkness Echoing" takes its title and its shape from "Personal Helicon" by Seamus Heaney.

Acknowledgments

5 A.M.: "Father," "Anger";

At Length: "Layoff";

The Awl: "To an Editor Who Said I Repeat Myself and Tell Too Much," "Variations on the Moment of Apprehending the Extent of One's Responsibilities";

Boston Review: "The Prince of Rivers";

Catch Up: "Narcissus and Me";

Colorado Review: "On His Bed and No Longer Among the Living," "My Mom, d. 1994," "Late Poem";

The Laurel Review: "Beginnings for an Essay in Spite of Itself";

The Literary Review: "Grief: A Celebration";

Maine: "Jazz";

The Nation: "Get Out";

The New Yorker: "Money Time";

Pleiades: "The Darkness Echoing," "It Came from the Primordial Ooze."

Thank you to Stephen Burt, Rob Casper, Erika Kawalik, Dennis Nurske, Parul Sehgal, Peter Conners and all at BOA, Stephanie G'Shwind, Monica de la Torre for pointing me to the paintings of Jorge Queiroz, and to Jorge Queiroz and the Sikkema Jenkins & Co. gallery for generously granting permission to use the stunning painting on the cover of this book. Thanks, too, to Dana Levin, D. A. Powell, all at *PW*, and my family.

Thank you to the Corporation of Yaddo and the MacDowell Colony for residencies during which much of this book was written.

About the Author

Craig Morgan Teicher is also the author of *Brenda Is in the Room and Other Poems*, chosen by Paul Hoover for the 2007 Colorado Prize for Poetry, and *Cradle Book*, named a notable book by the Story Prize committee. His poems have appeared in the *New Yorker*, the *Nation*, the *Paris Review*, the *Best American Poetry*, and many other publications. He works at *Publishers Weekly* and serves as an editor for the *Literary Review*. His writing about books, authors, and technology is published widely, and he has served on the board of the National Book Critics Circle. He lives in Brooklyn, New York, with his wife and children.

BOA EDITIONS, LTD. AMERICAN POETS CONTINUUM SERIES

Colophon

To Keep Love Blurry, poems by Craig Morgan Teicher,
is set in Adobe Garamond, a digital font designed in 1989
by Robert Slimbach (1956–) based on the French Renaissance roman
types of Claude Garamond (ca. 1480–1561) and the italics of
Robert Granjon (1513–1589).

The publication of this book is made possible, in part,
by the special support of the following individuals:

Anonymous
Romolo Celli
Anne Germanacos
X. J. & Dorothy M. Kennedy
Jack & Gail Langerak
Katherine Lederer
Boo Poulin
Deborah Ronnen & Sherm Levey
Steven O Russell & Phyllis Rifkin Russell
Ellen & David Wallack
Glenn & Helen William